FLOWER POWER

The Art of Coloring

Adult Coloring Book

This book is full of great things to color. Coloring relaxes and helps with stress and

Anxiety. Landscapes is easy to color and be creative. A Great Pass time.

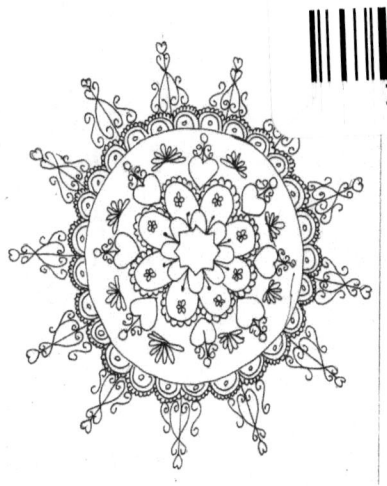

I0475846

Pocket edition

The Artist Korner

Heflin, AL 36264

Printed in U.S.A

The Artist Korner

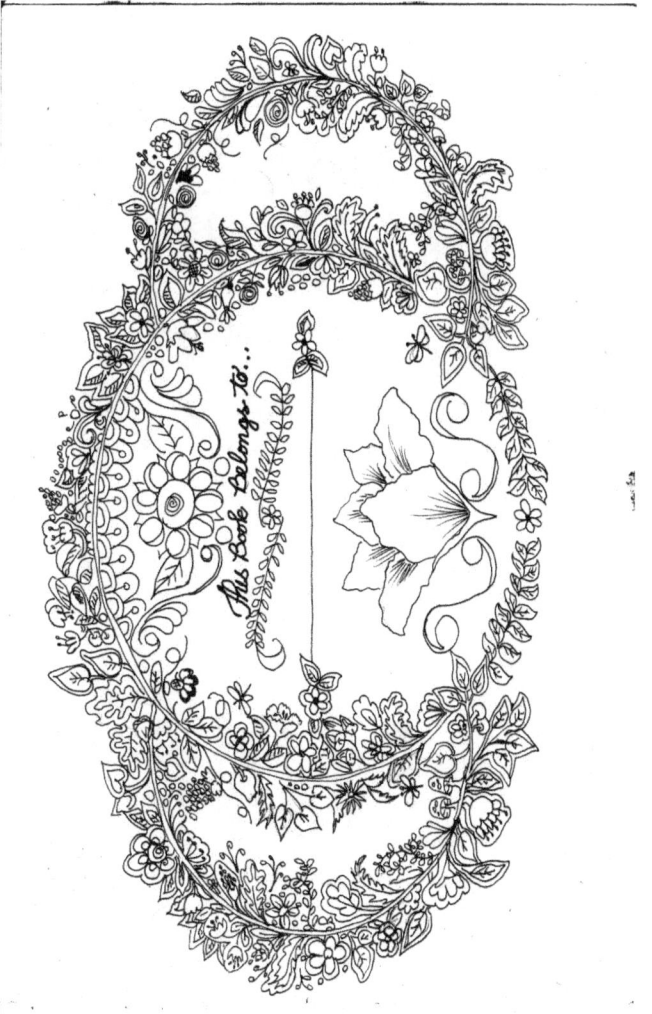

This Book Belongs To...

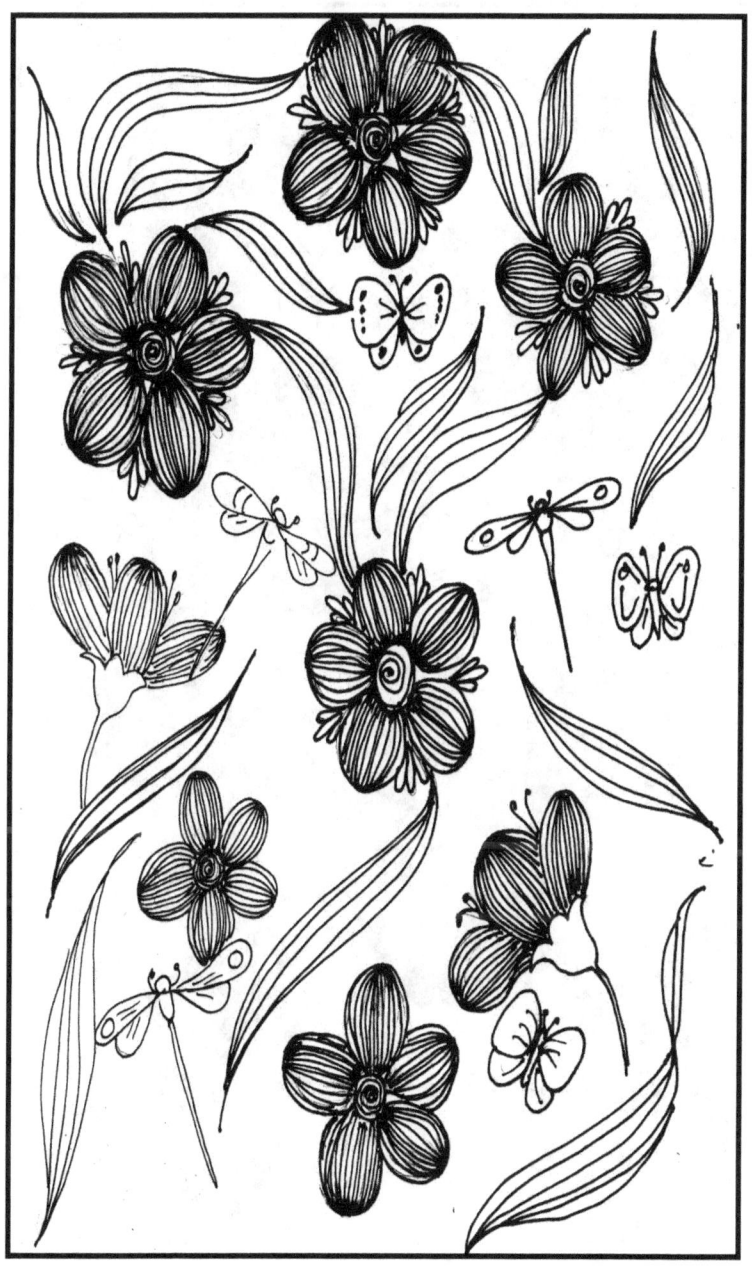

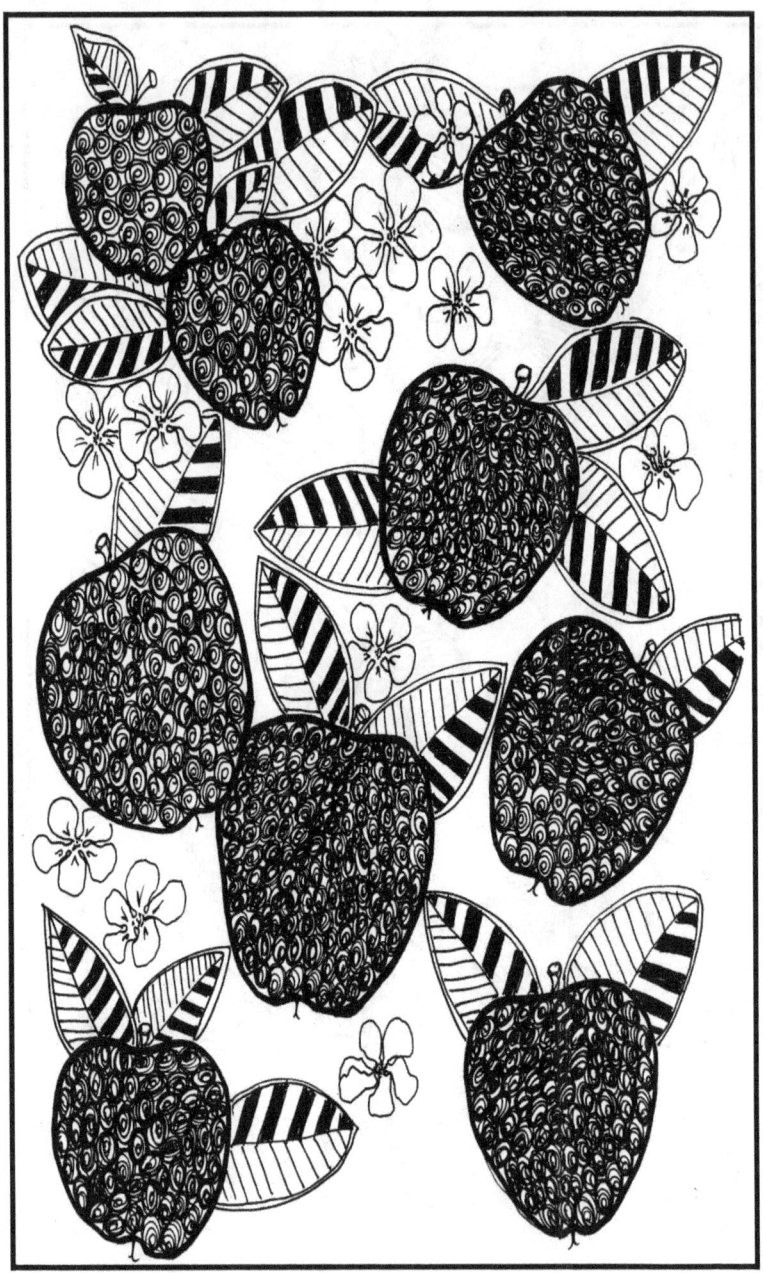

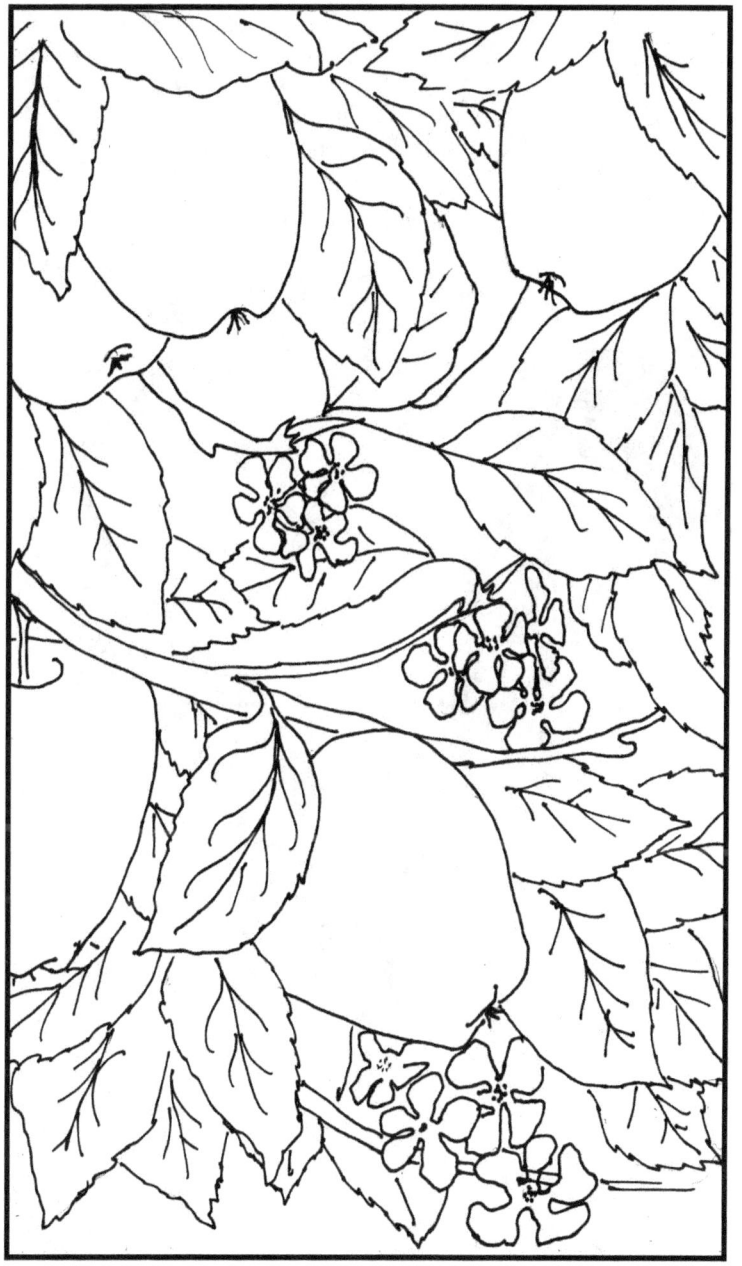

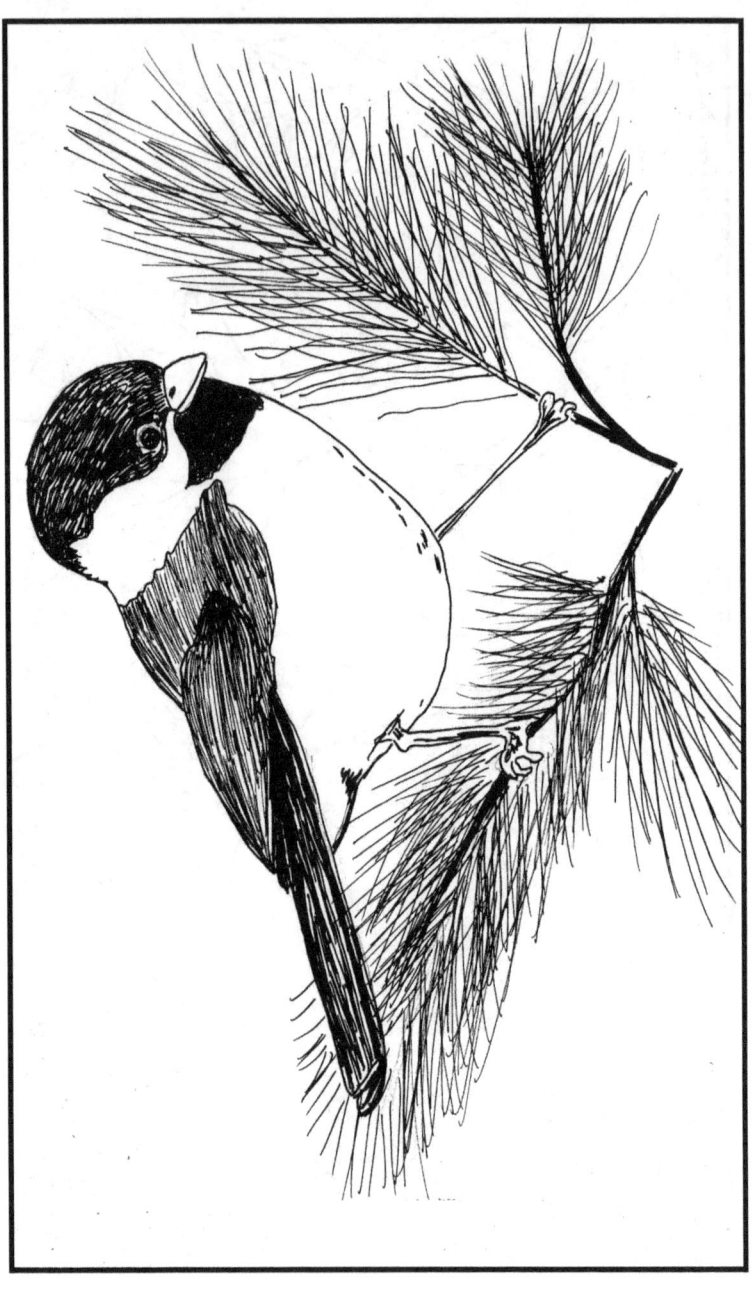

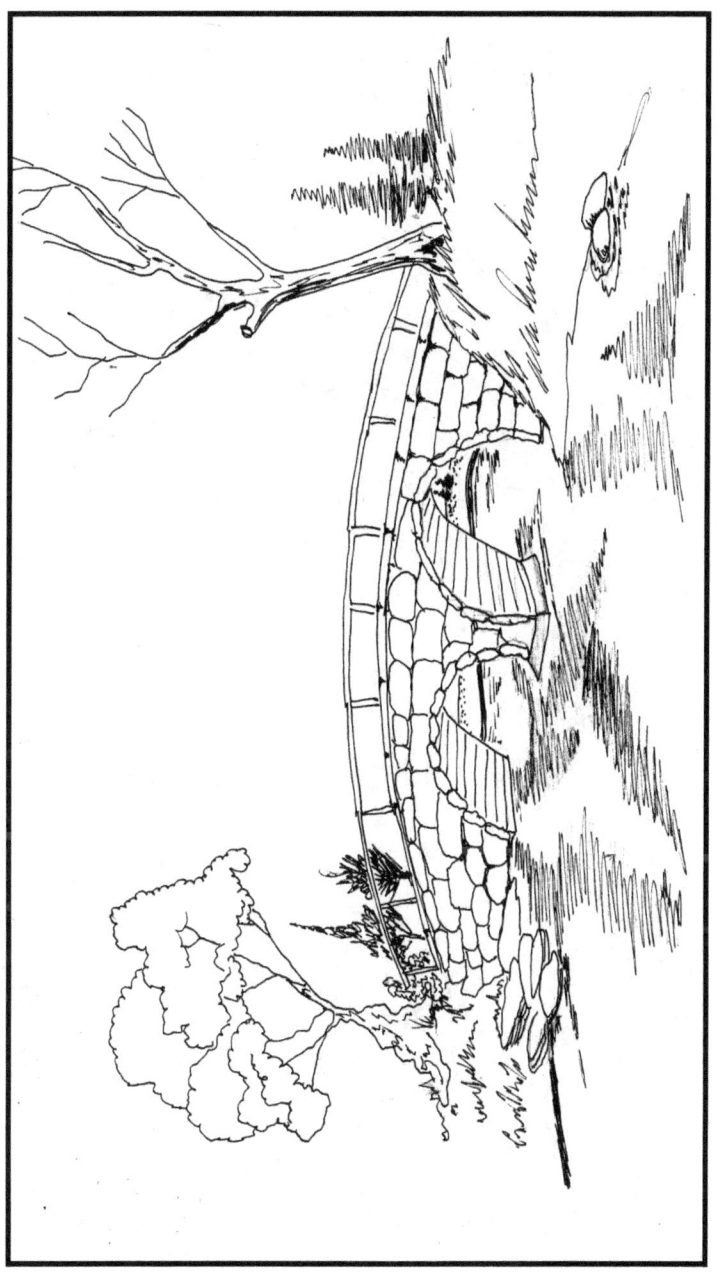

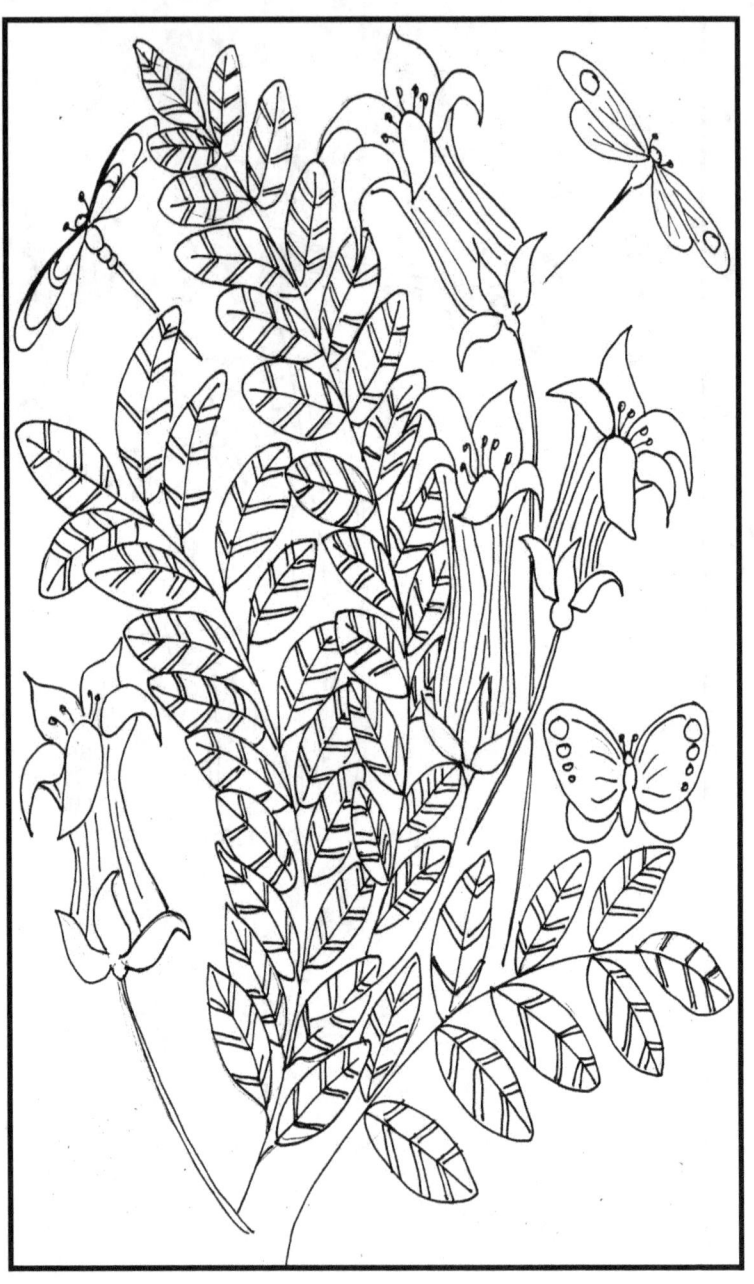

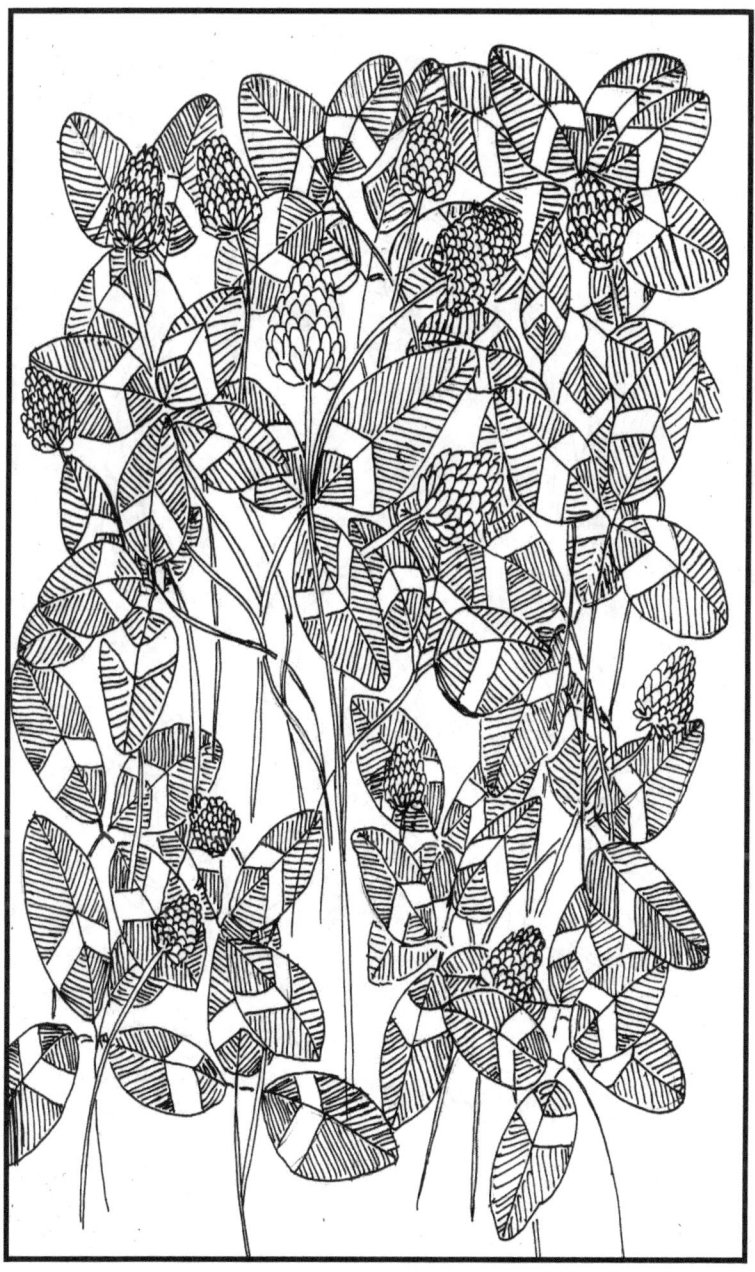

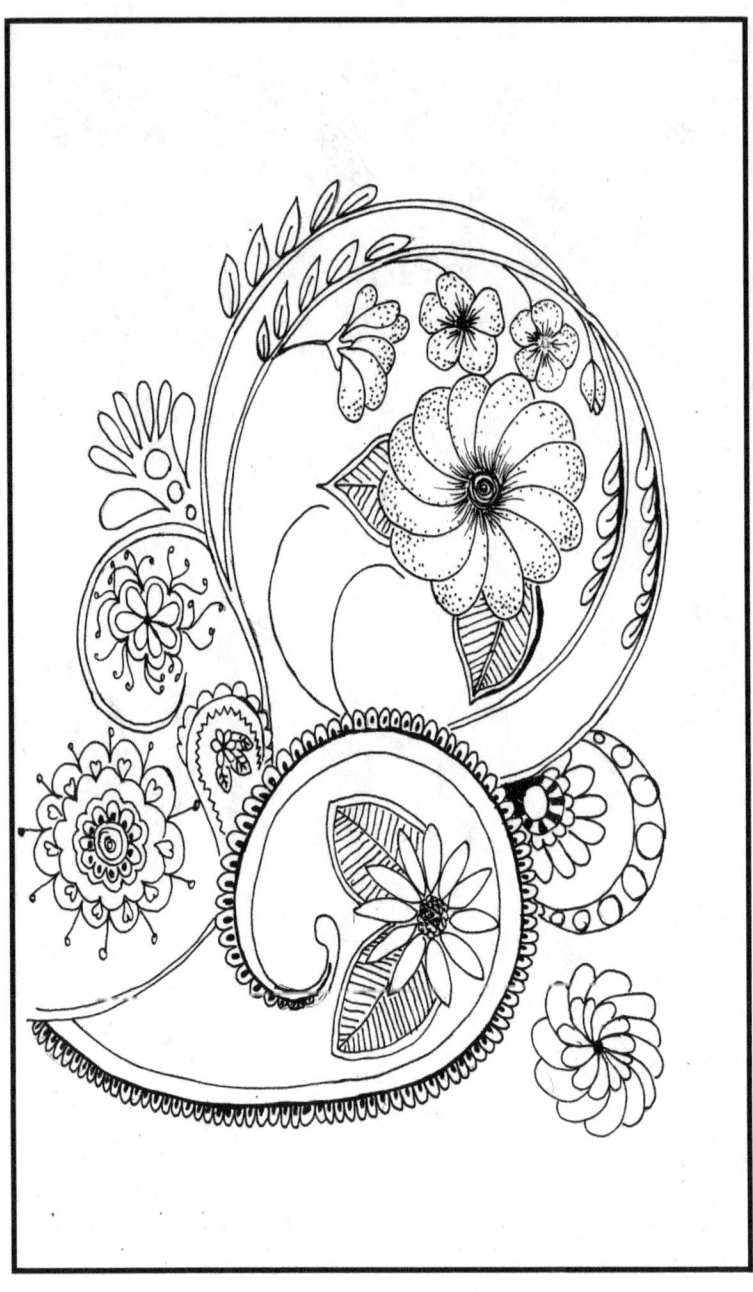

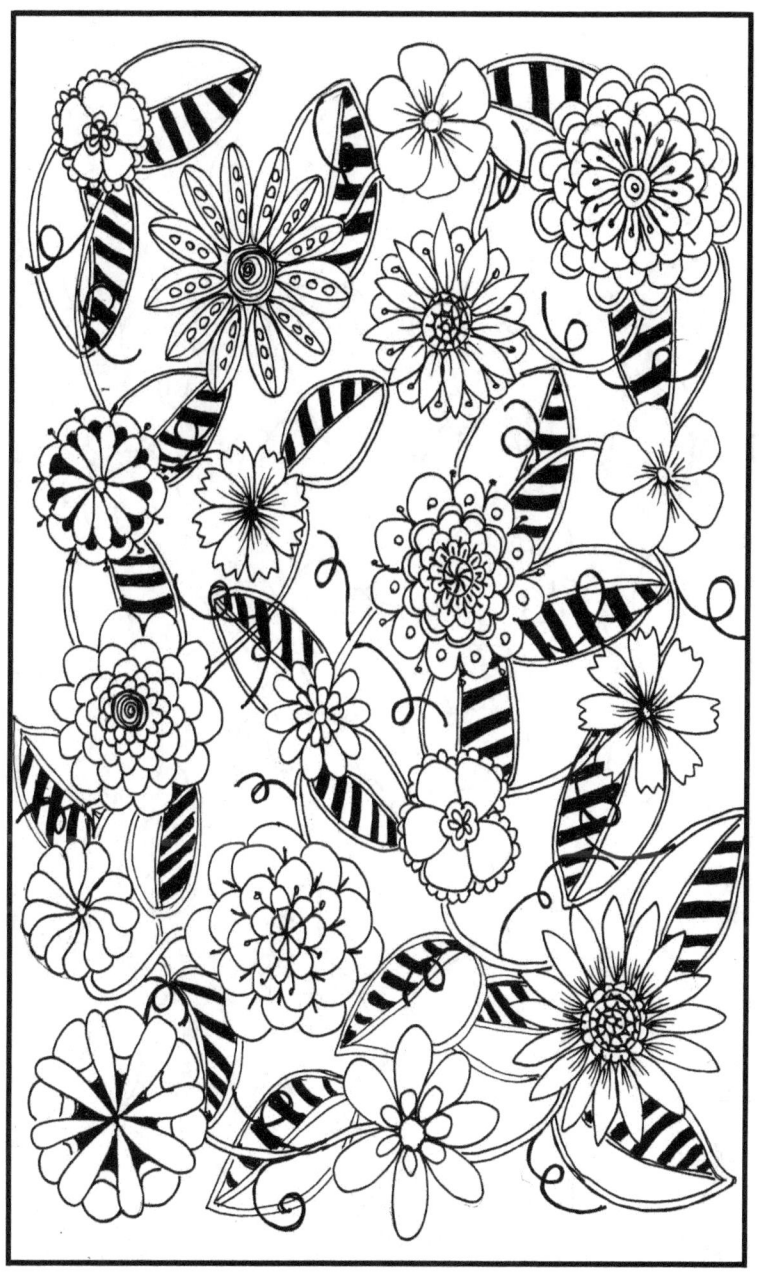

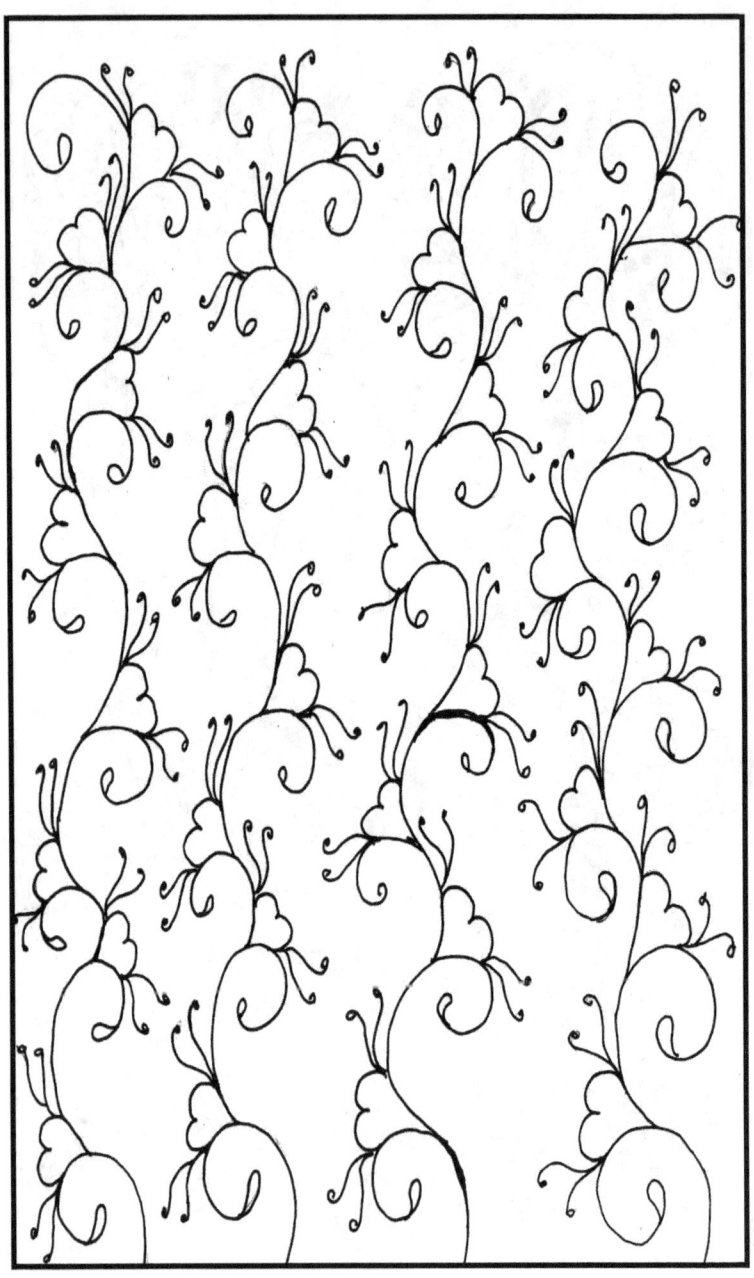

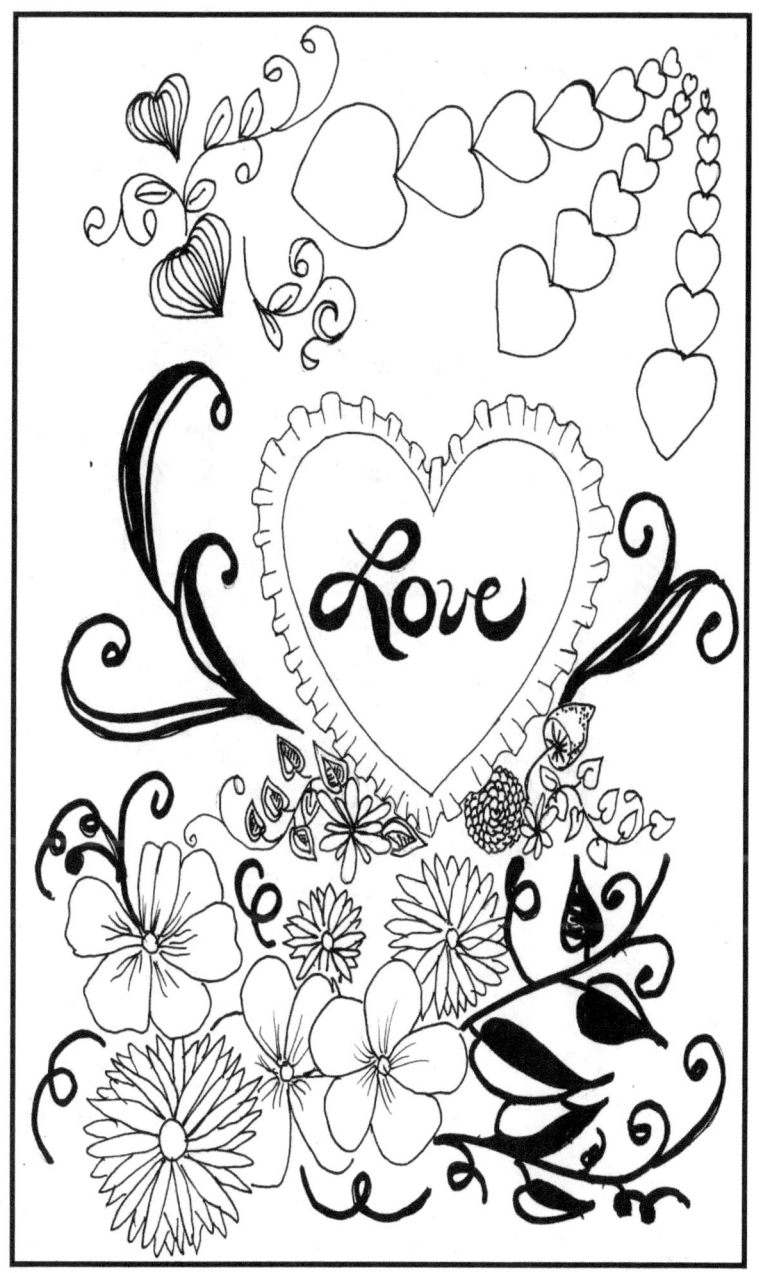

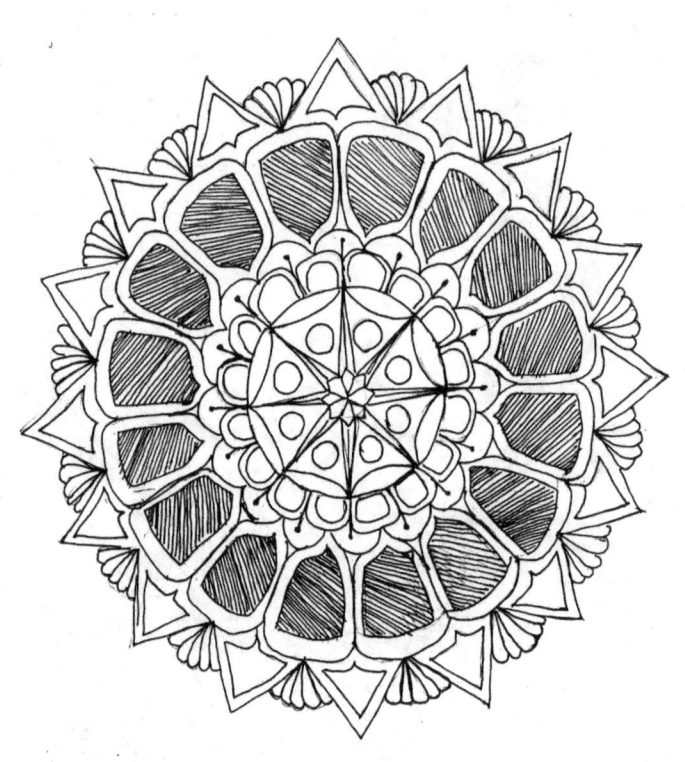

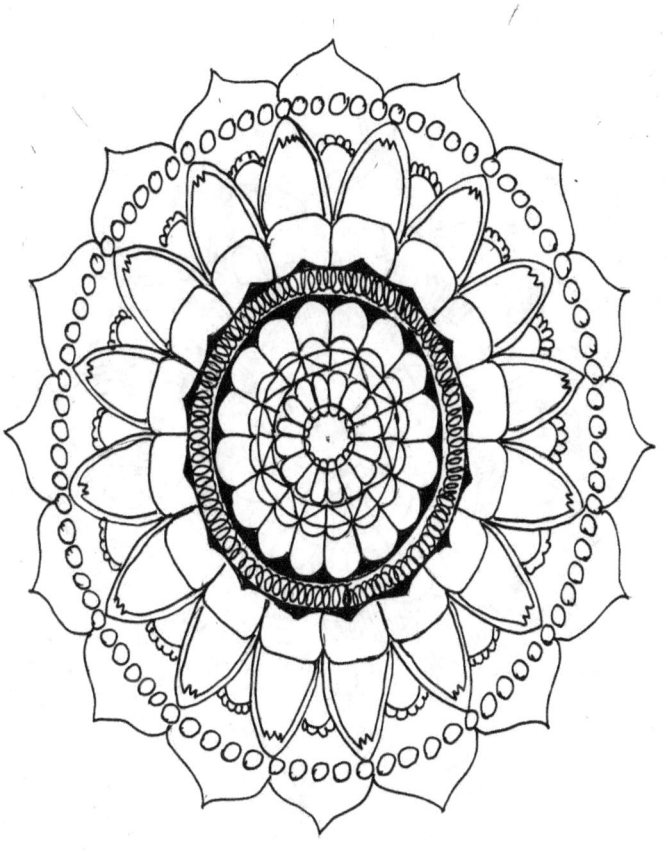

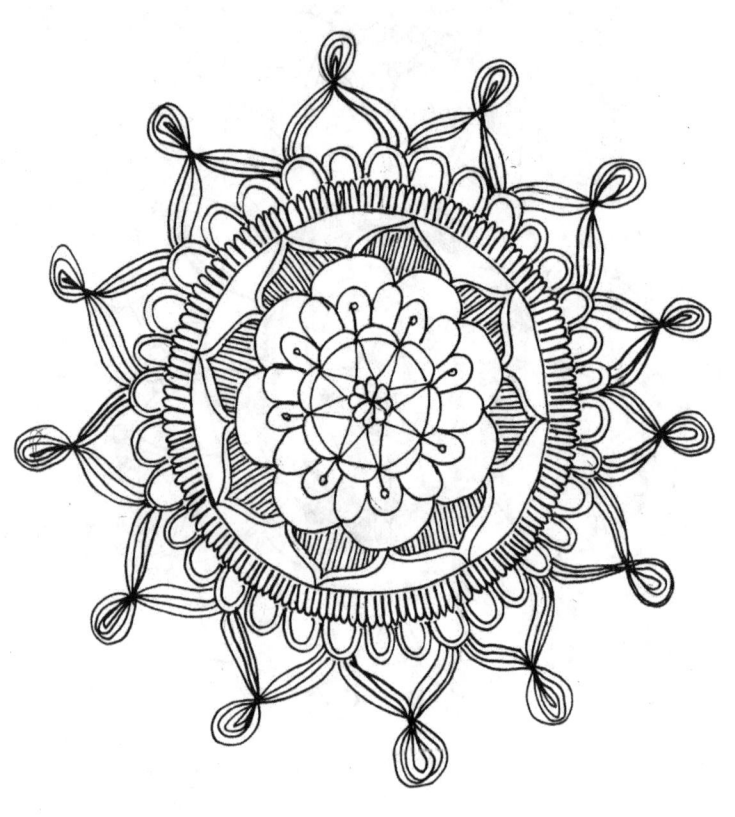

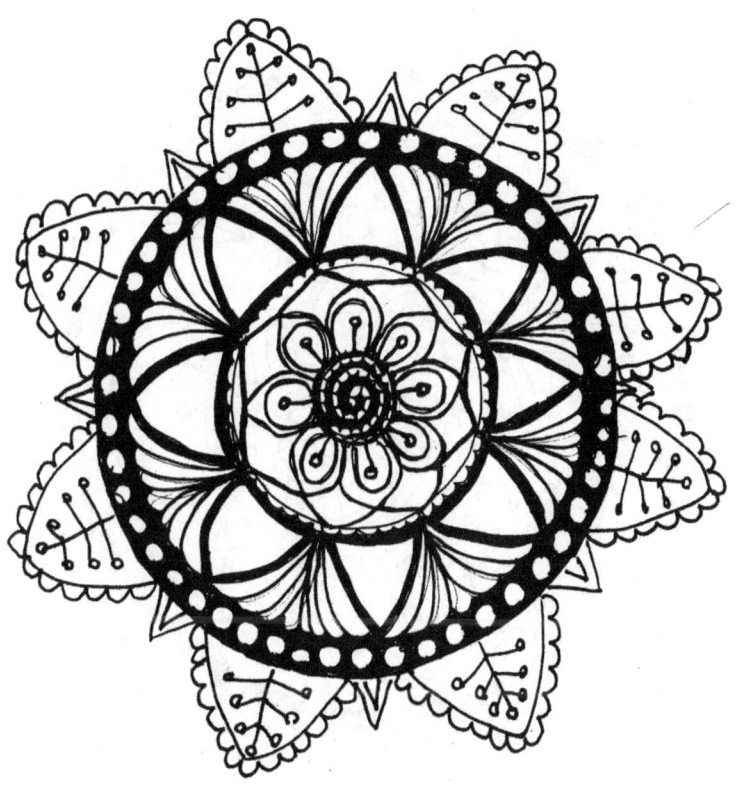

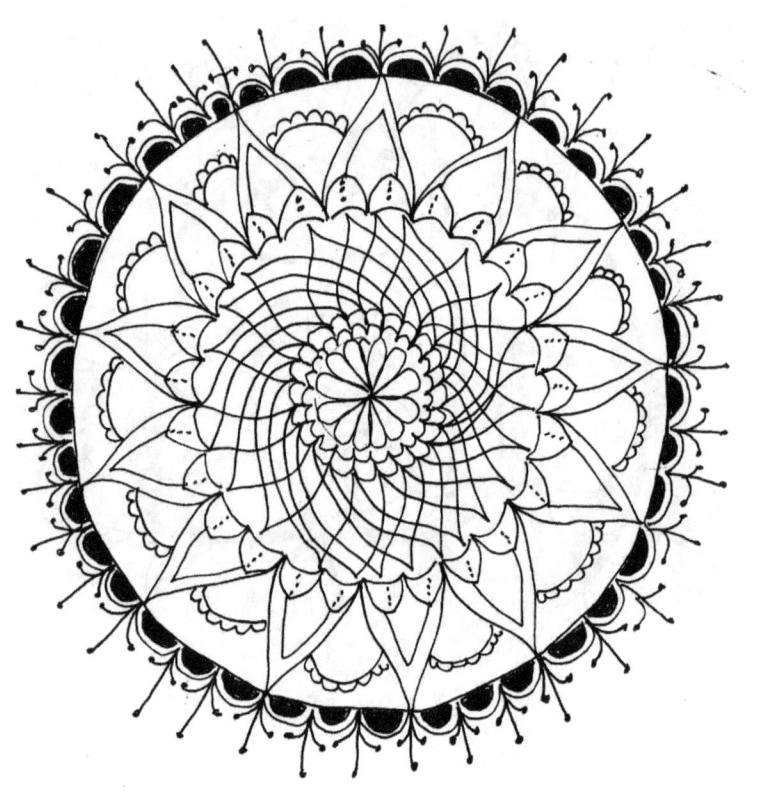

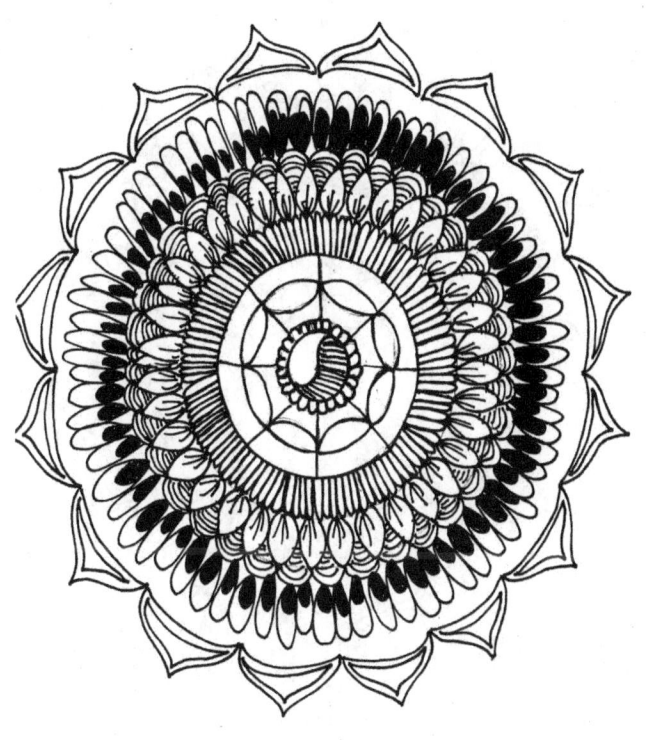

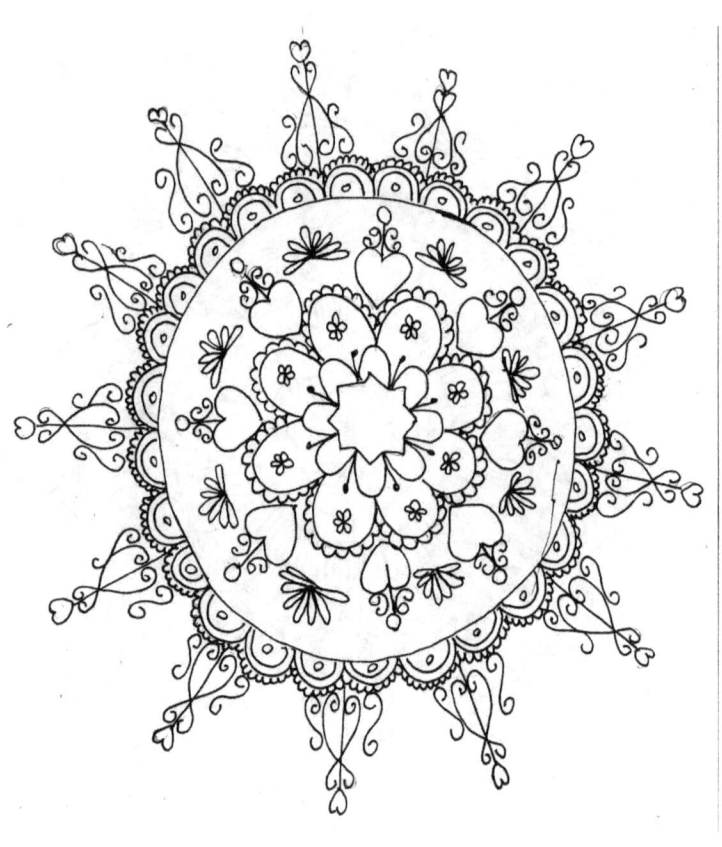

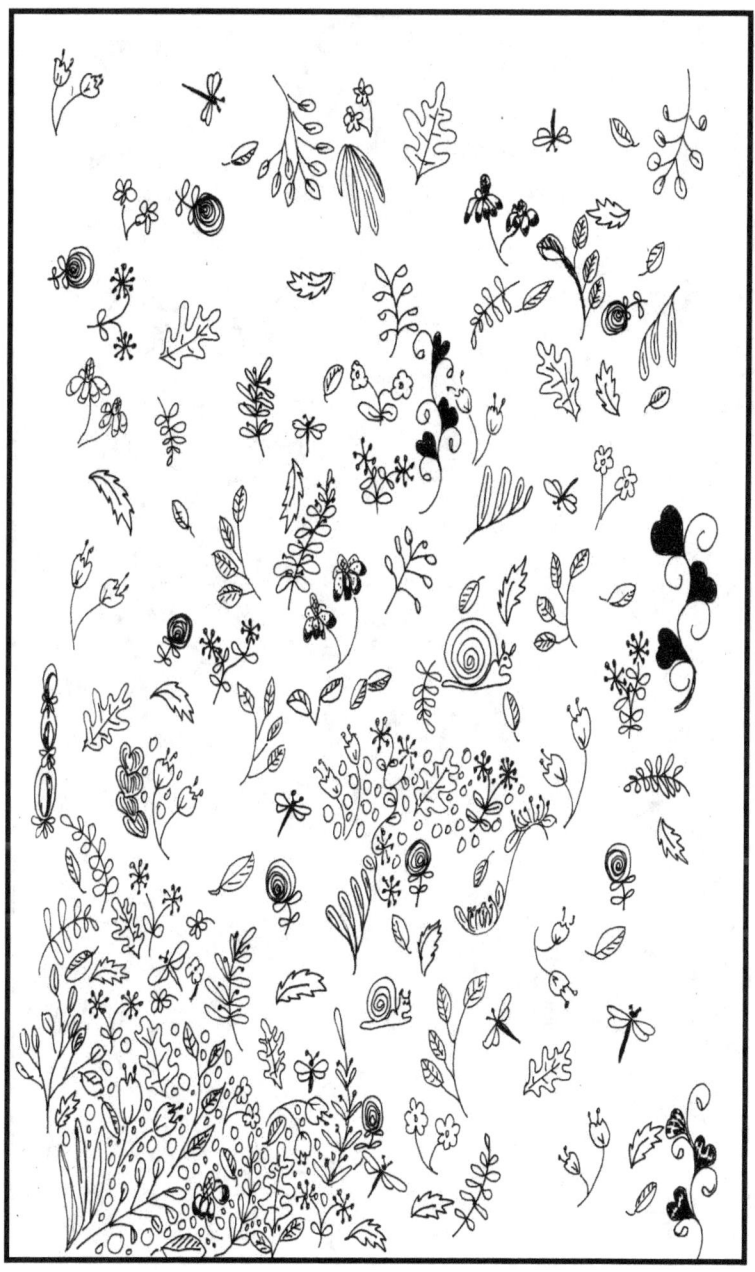

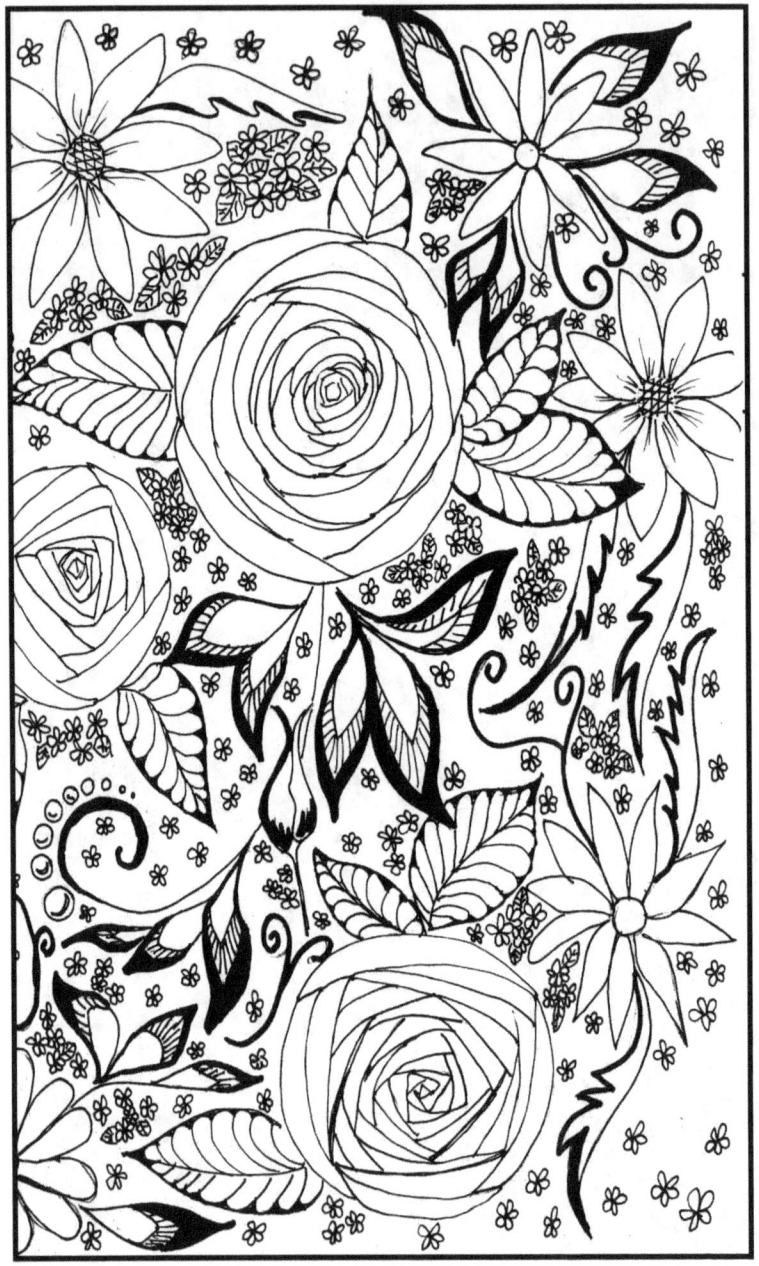

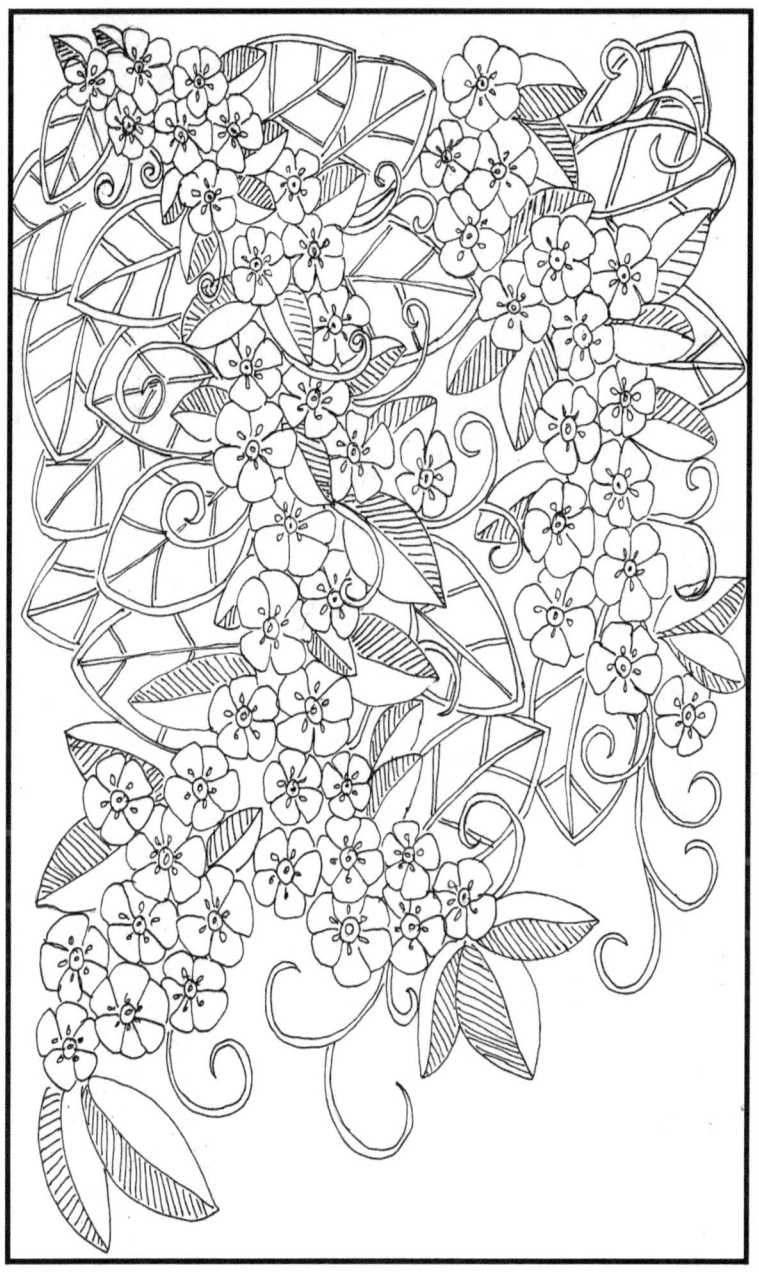

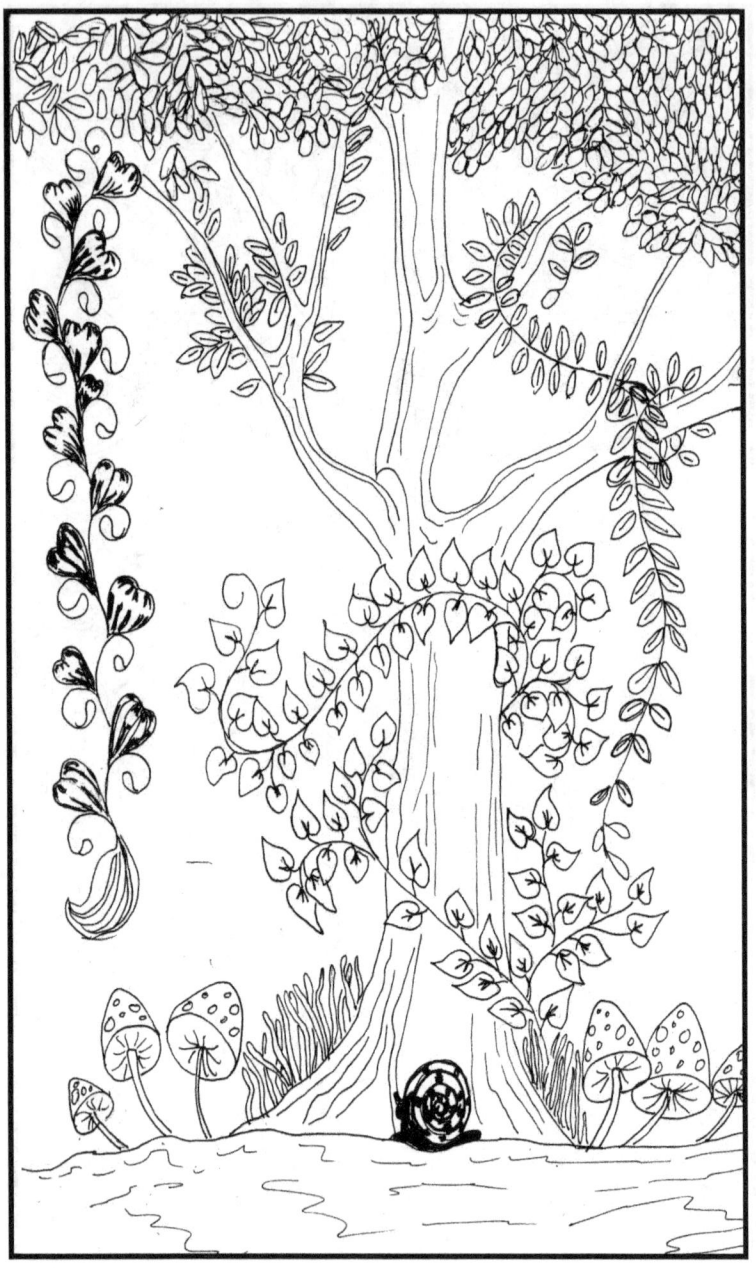

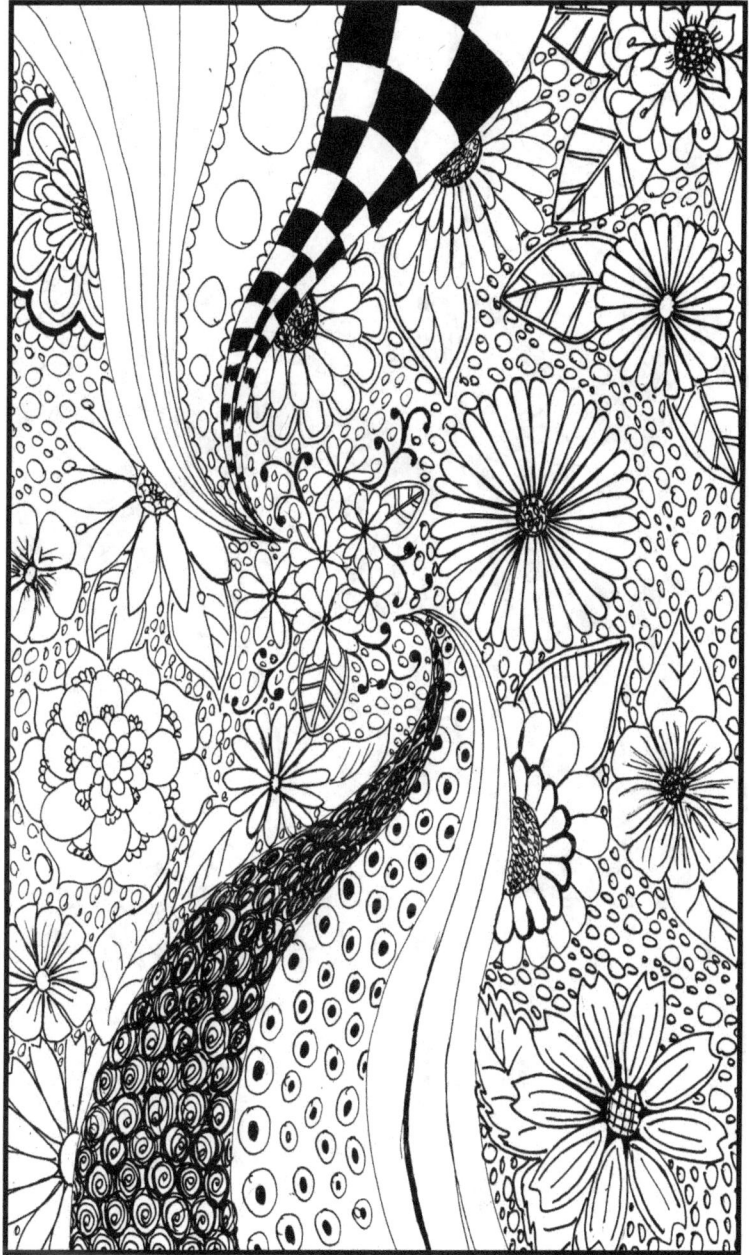

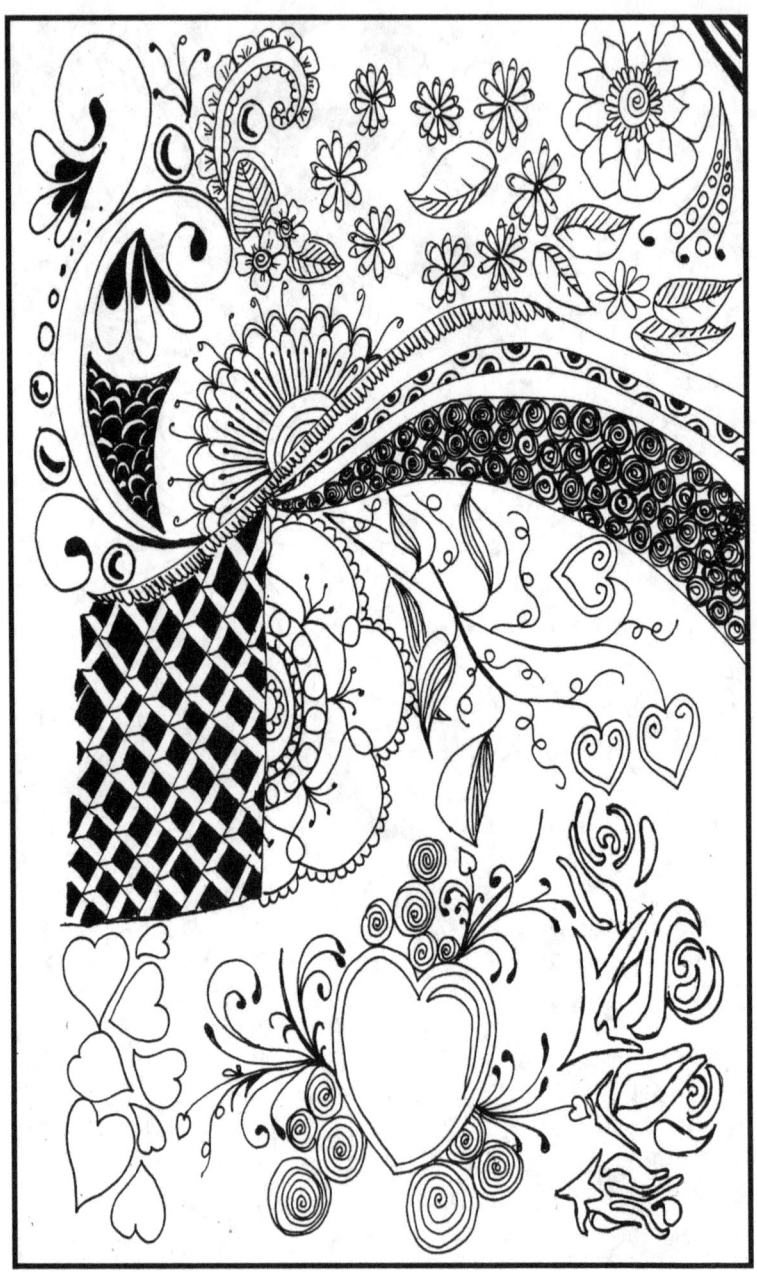

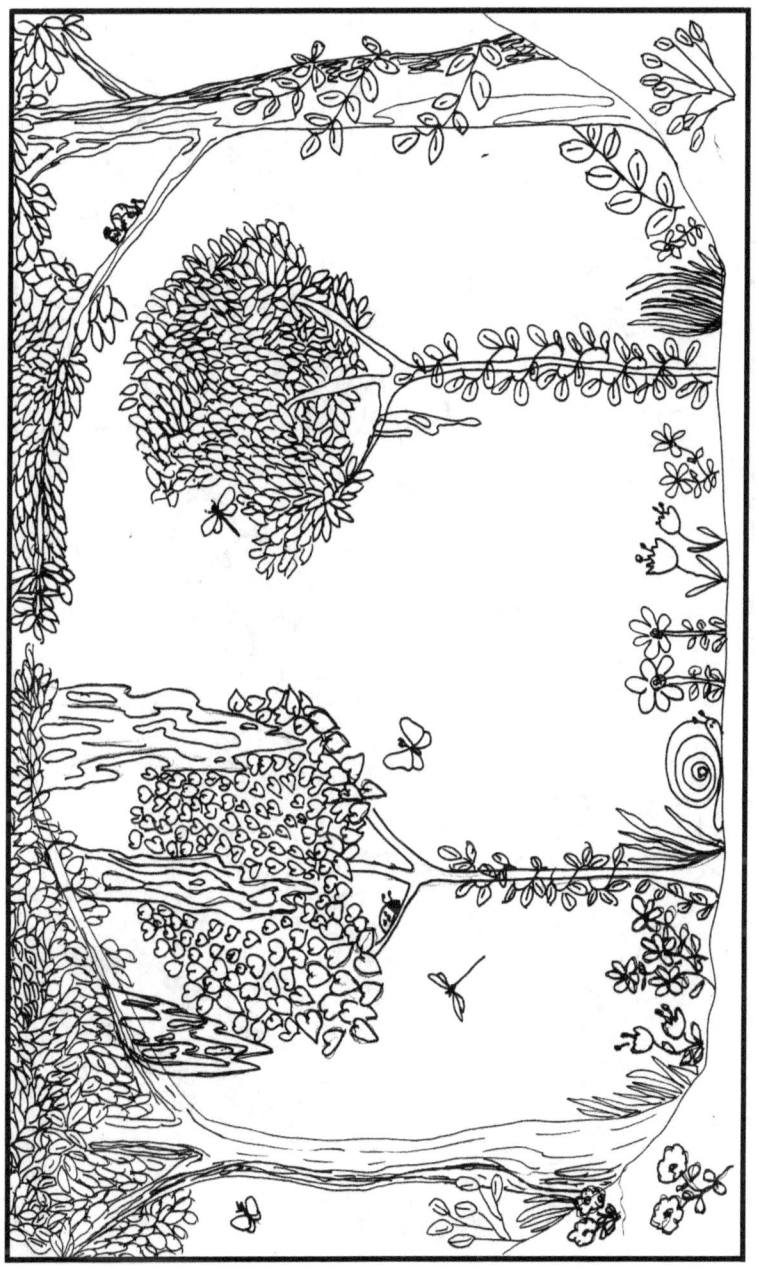

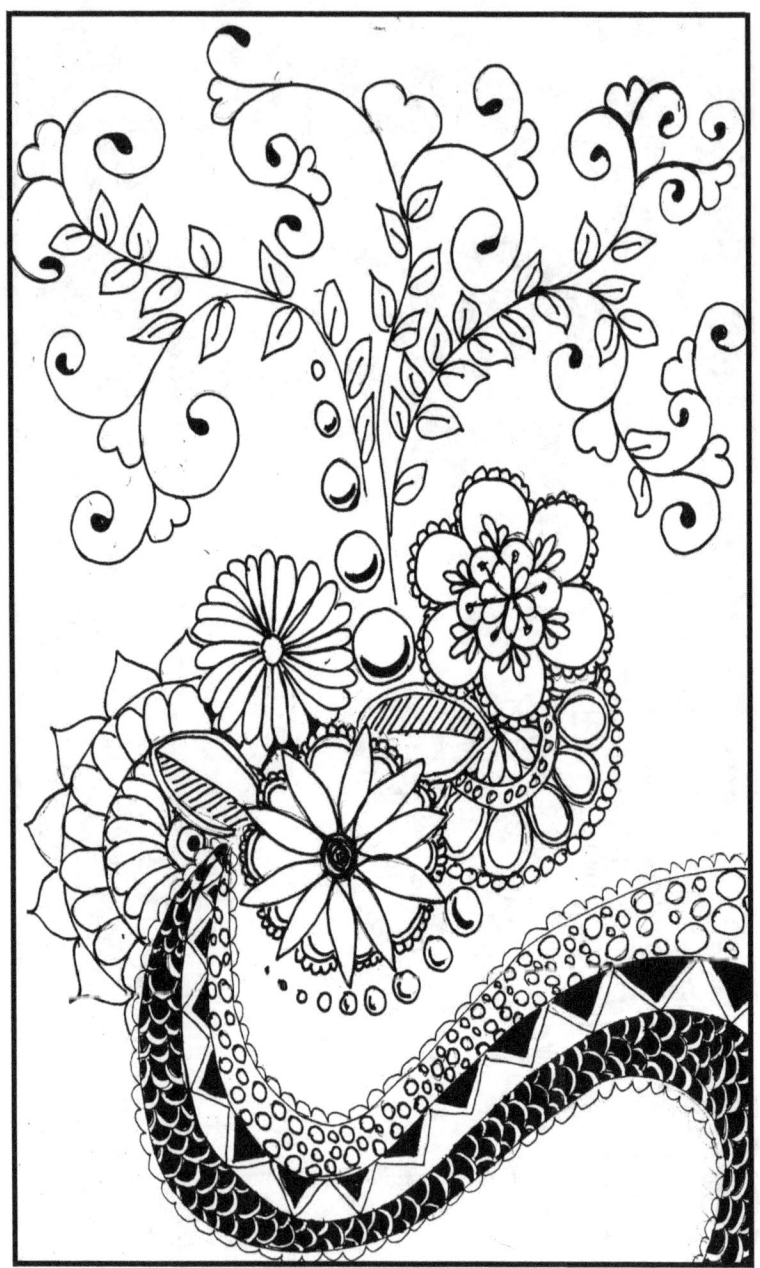

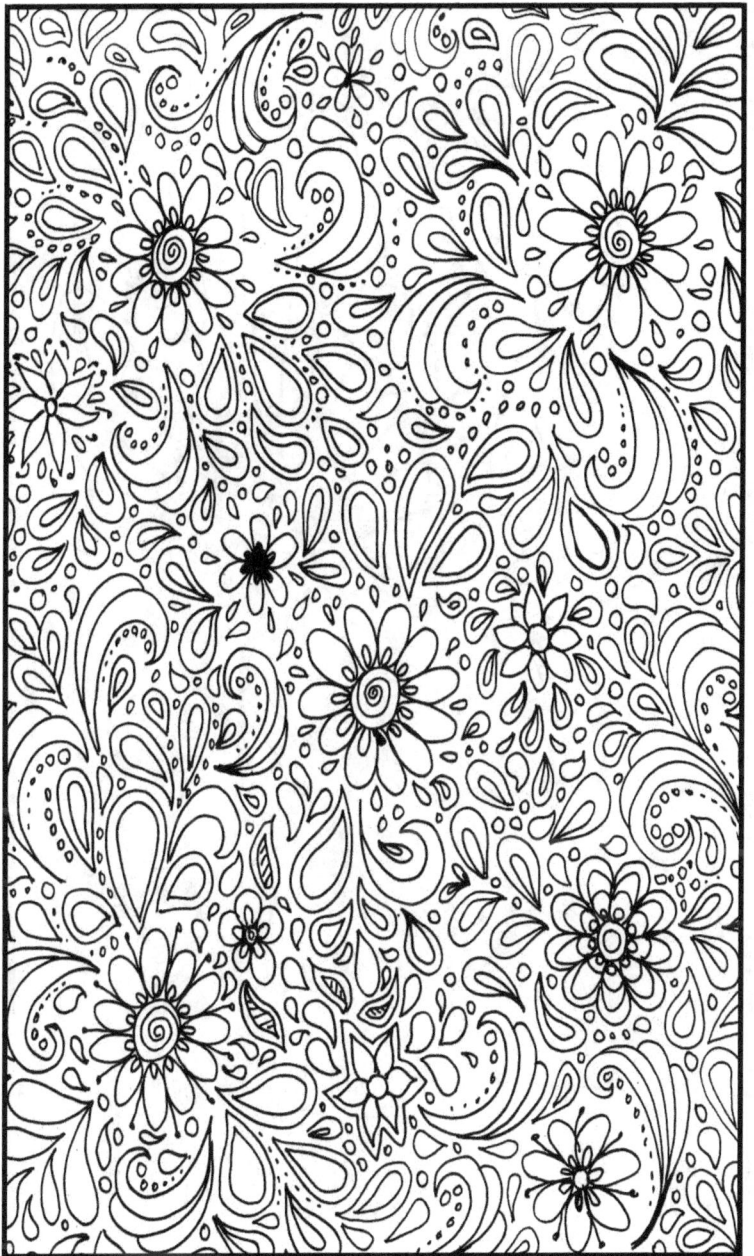

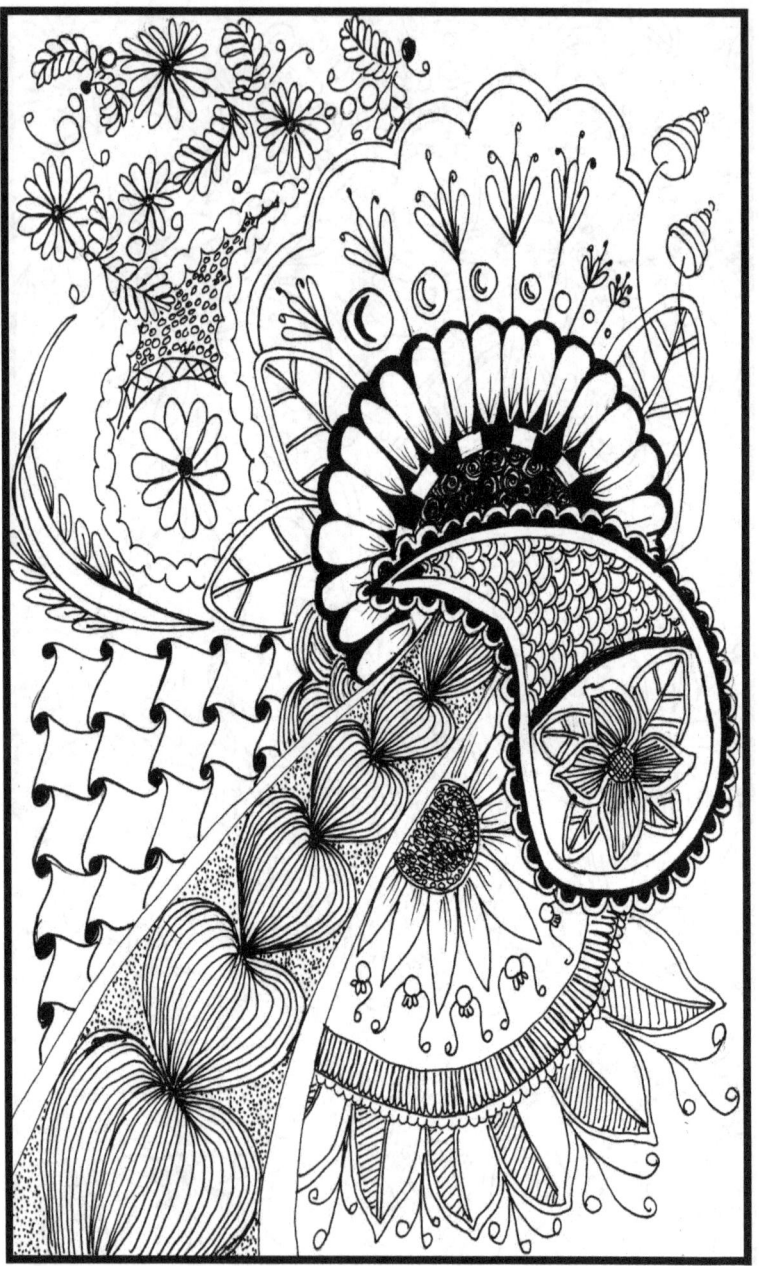

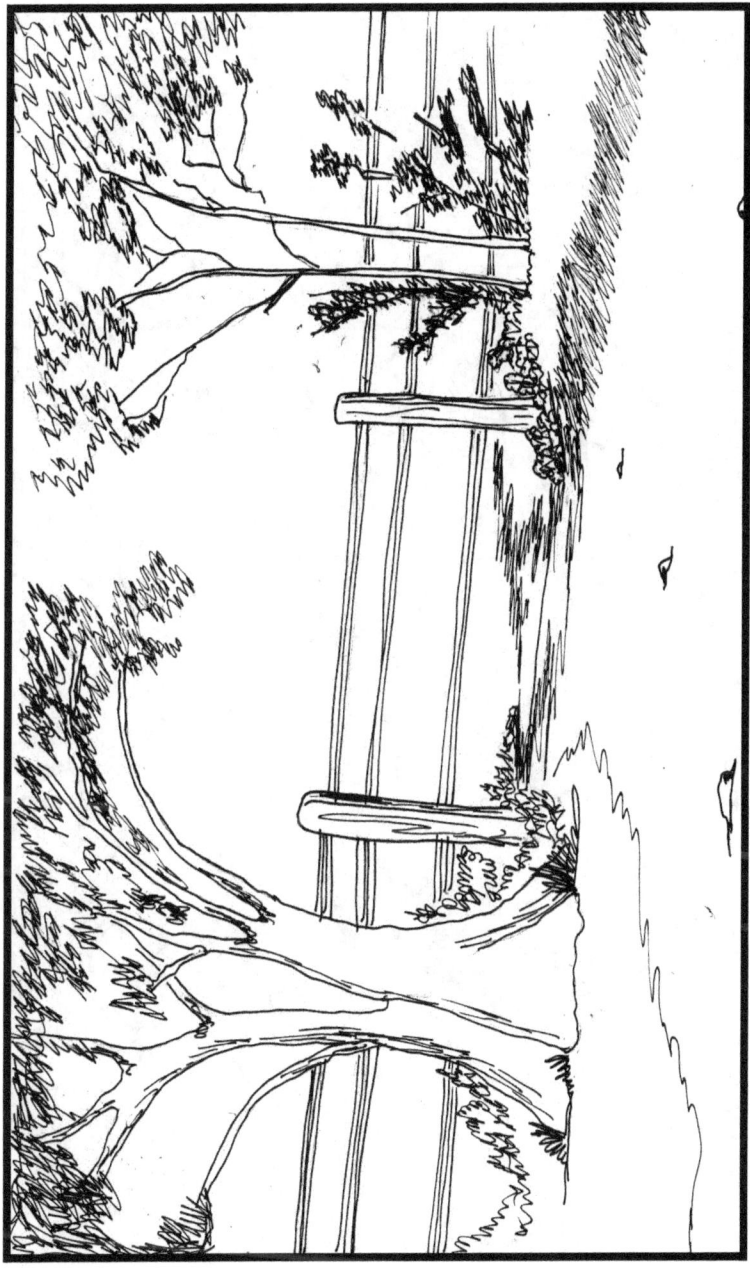

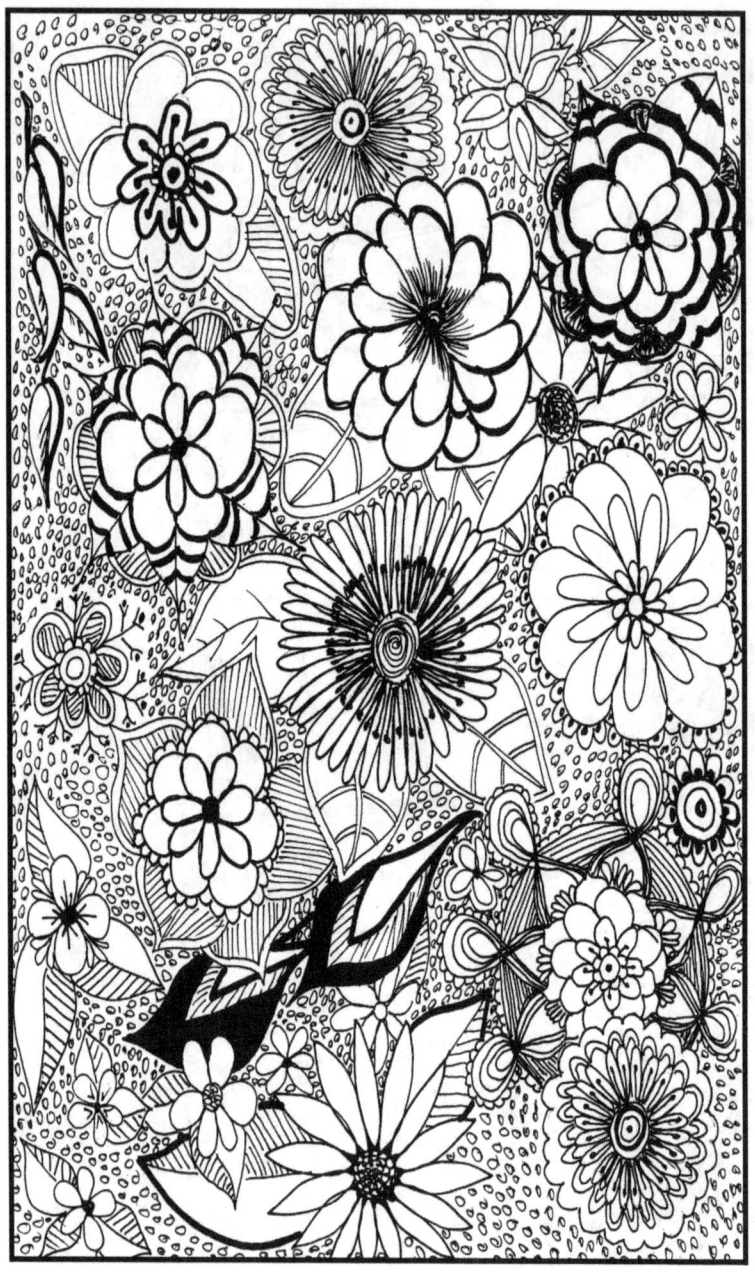

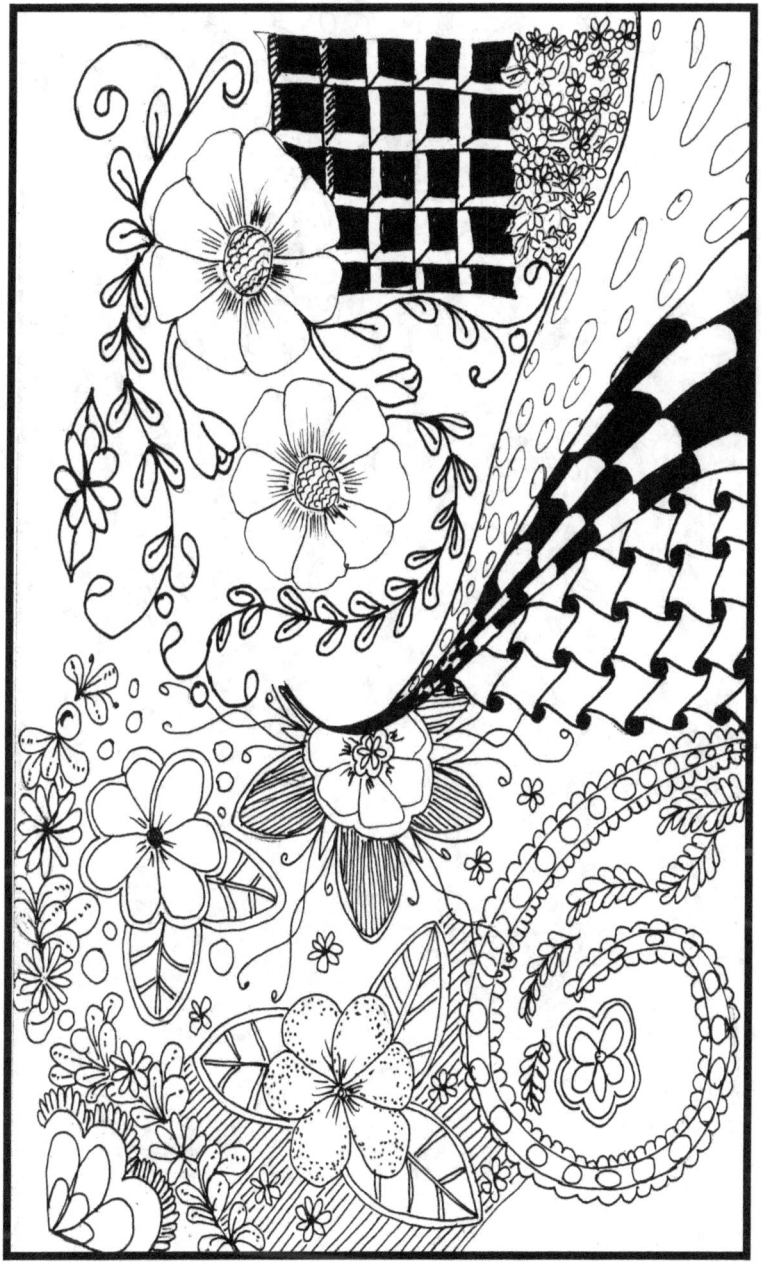

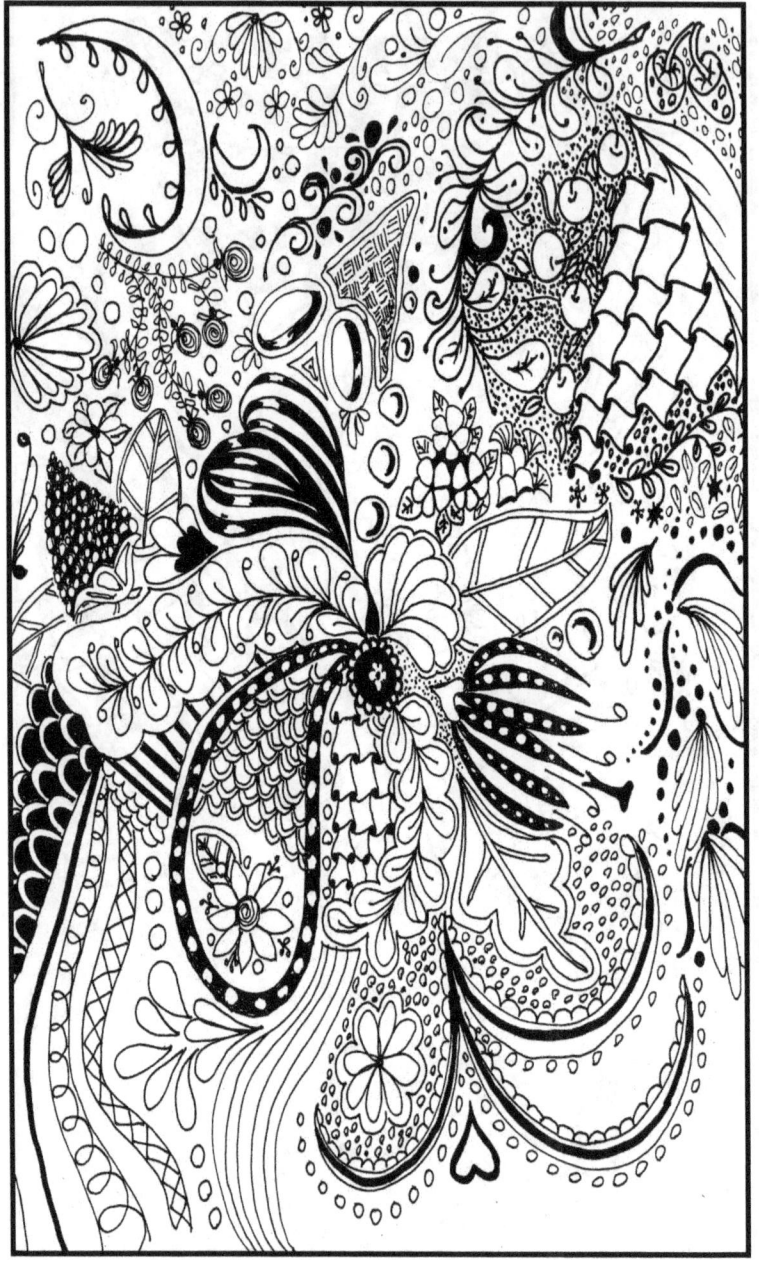

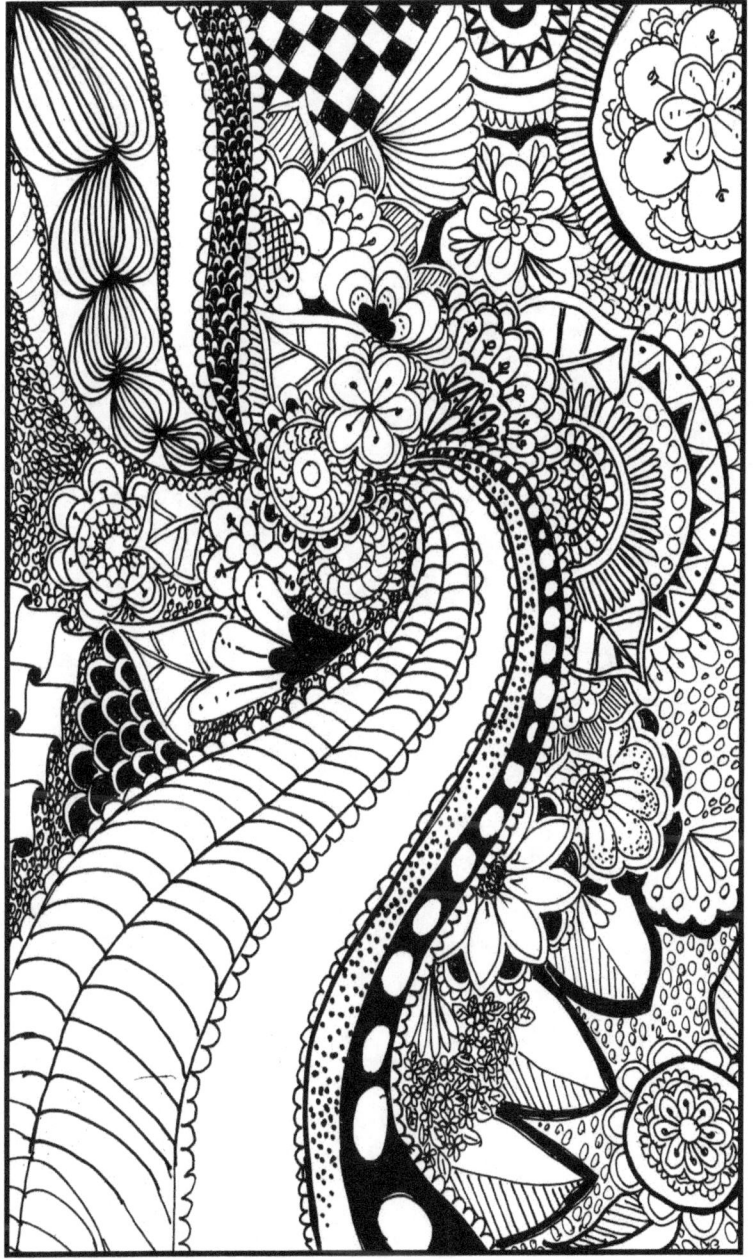